GREEN TURTLE

NATIONAL
GEOGRAPHIC
KiDS

GO WILD!
Sea Turtles

Jill Esbaum

NATIONAL GEOGRAPHIC
WASHINGTON, D.C.

Graceful glider.
Seagrass nibbler.
Mollusk muncher.

That's a sea turtle!
These swimmy reptiles travel the
world's oceans.

Come along!

Life in the Shallows

Most sea turtles like living in warm shallow water near coastlines and coral reefs. That's where it's easy to find their favorite foods. But if hunting is easier a little farther from shore, off they go!

GREEN TURTLE

HAWKSBILL

GREEN TURTLE

When they're tired, sea turtles take a floaty nap on top of the waves or swim down to snooze under rocky ledges.

Ahhh.

Cozy Coastlines

Sea turtles live in all oceans except the Arctic. That water is too cold! Here are a few popular places to spot sea turtles:

Hawaii
This U.S. state is made up of eight main islands.

Mexico
This large country has many kinds of animal habitats, including oceans, deserts, rainforests, and mountains.

Costa Rica
This small country has seven active volcanoes!

NORTH AMERICA

Mexico

↑ Hawaii

Costa Rica

SOUTH AMERICA

PACIFIC OCEAN

ARCTIC OCEAN

EUROPE

ASIA

AFRICA

PACIFIC
OCEAN

Malaysia

INDIAN
OCEAN

ATLANTIC
OCEAN

**Great
Barrier
Reef**

AUSTRALIA

ANTARCTICA

Malaysia
**The two parts of this
country are separated
by a large body of
water called
the South
China Sea.**

The Great
Barrier Reef
**Earth's most famous reef
system is so big it can be
seen from space!**

So Big!

Different kinds of sea turtles grow to be different sizes. The smallest sea turtle is the Kemp's ridley. Though it is only about two feet (61 cm) long, it can weigh between 70 and 100 pounds (32 and 45 kg).

That's about as heavy as four car tires!

The biggest sea turtle is the leatherback. This turtle can be as long as seven feet (2 m)—that's as long as a sofa! It can weigh up to 2,000 pounds (900 kg).

That's as heavy as two horses!

Made for the Sea

Take a look at this green turtle. Each part of its body is perfect for an animal that lives and hunts in the ocean.

Short back flippers help with turning and stopping.

Hard upper and lower shells protect a soft body. Shells are bone covered with thin, platelike scales called scutes.

Sea turtles have clear underwater eyesight, but don't see well out of water.

No teeth here! Sea turtles break their food into smaller pieces with their beak.

Long front flippers are great for paddling!

A sensitive nose picks up smells from far away.

Ears are hidden under the skin behind a turtle's eyes. Turtles hear low sounds best.

Air In, Salt Out

Sea turtles need to breathe air.

While swimming and diving, they usually come to the surface to breathe every few minutes. All that moving around is a lot of work! But when they rest in one place, they can stay underwater much longer.

Sea turtles eat food from the ocean. It's salty! They also drink salty ocean water. Too much salt isn't healthy for their bodies, so some needs to come out. How? It leaks out through their eyes!

GREEN TURTLE

Meet the Family!

Seven kinds of sea turtles swim in the world's oceans.

Flatback

These turtles live only near Australia and Papua New Guinea. Can you guess how they got their name? That's one flat back!

Green turtle

These turtles are the largest of all hard-shelled turtles. Their fat is green!

Kemp's ridley

While most female turtles lay their eggs alone, these turtles come onto a beach in big groups and lay their eggs together.

Hawksbill

These turtles got their name from the shape of their mouth, which is like a hawk's beak.

Leatherback

Female leatherbacks swim farther than any other sea turtle. To get from their eating places to their nesting beaches, they can travel 4,000 miles (6,400 km) or more.

Olive ridley

These turtles are very much like their Kemp's ridley relatives, but their shells form a higher peak.

Loggerhead

Big head? Check. As big as a log? Well, maybe not. But people say that's how these sea turtles got their name.

Hello, Leatherback!

Unlike other sea turtles, the leatherback does not have a shell. Instead, it has small bones covered by thick skin that feels rubbery—like the bottom of your sneakers. It can even bend a little. A thick layer of fat under this shell helps a leatherback stay warm, even in cold water.

The leatherback dives deeper than any other sea turtle— more than 4,000 feet (1 km)! And while paddling around way down there in the deep, it can hold its breath for nearly an hour and a half.

What's on the Menu?

Hmm, what's for dinner today? That depends on what kind of sea turtle is hungry! Some eat shelled creatures like crabs, mussels, shrimps, and snails.

LOGGERHEAD EATING LOBSTER

HAWKSBILL EATING JELLYFISH

Others eat mostly jellyfish.

GREEN TURTLE EATING SEAWEED

Some sea turtles prefer plants. They graze on swaying seagrass or nibble algae growing on coral reefs.

Munch! Munch!

Each kind of sea turtle has a mouth just right for what it likes to eat.

A green turtle has jagged jaws, good for tearing off seagrass.

GREEN TURTLE EATING SEAGRASS

HAWKSBILL
EATING CORAL

A hawksbill has a pointy beak, good for picking sea sponges from cracks and crevices in coral reefs.

LOGGERHEAD EATING TRUMPET SHELL

A loggerhead has very strong jaws, good for cracking shelled creatures.

23

Home to Nest

Every one to five years, an adult female sea turtle swims back to the beach where she hatched. Sometimes that beach is across the ocean!

She crawls onto shore at night and digs a hole with her back flippers. This is her nest. She lays eggs into the nest and covers them with sand. Then she returns to the ocean.

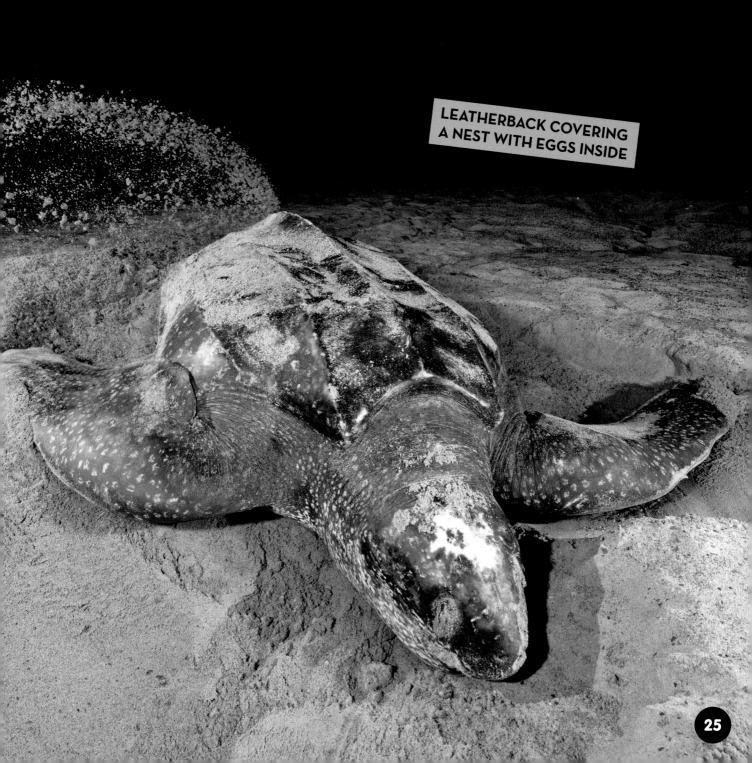

LEATHERBACK COVERING A NEST WITH EGGS INSIDE

Safe and Snug

Each nest may have more than 100 eggs. After about two months buried in the sand, a baby begins tap-tap-tapping at its shell. To break the shell, it uses a special tooth called an egg tooth, which falls out a few days later.

LEATHERBACK EGGS

A group of eggs in a sea turtle's nest is called a clutch.

LEATHERBACK HATCHLING

The baby wriggles from its broken shell, but it doesn't crawl out of the sand just yet. Instead, it waits ... and waits ... until almost every egg in the clutch is hatched. This can take as many as seven days! When all the babies are ready, they work together to dig out of the sand.

Ready, Set, GO!

One night, after dark, the hatchlings pop up all at once and rush to the ocean as fast as their tiny flippers will carry them.

A PHOTOGRAPHER USES LIGHT TO TAKE A PHOTO OF LEATHERBACK HATCHLINGS AT NIGHT.

Why are they in such a hurry?
Because predators like crabs, birds, foxes, and raccoons want to catch and eat them.

Swimming in Seaweed

The turtle babies swim to clumps of seaweed that float far out in the ocean.

They stay there for many months, gobbling plants and tiny sea animals. These foods help them

grow, grow, grow!

Female turtles will someday go back to the beach to lay their own eggs. But male turtles will never return to shore again.

LOGGERHEAD

A Green Turtle's Life

2 months–3 years: Scientists believe green turtles spend up to three years living in big clumps of floating seaweed.

0–2 months: A green turtle grows inside its egg. Then it breaks out and races to the ocean.

20–50 years:

Sometime during these years, females begin laying eggs. They make nests every one to five years. Males swim to find females near the beaches where they lay their eggs.

3–20 years:

Green turtles live in shallow waters, eating seagrass and algae.

80 years:

Green turtles can live 80 years or more. What a wonderful, swimmy life!

Turtle scutes are made of keratin, just like human fingernails.

Some sea turtles can live more than 100 years.

A leatherback snags its favorite food—jellyfish—with its hooked beak. Once that happens, the jelly can't escape. Chomp!

Sea turtles have been around since the time of dinosaurs.

34

Sea turtles ride the ocean currents like watery highways. Wheee!

When a sea turtle is underwater for a long time, its heart might beat only once every nine minutes!

Unlike land turtles, sea turtles cannot pull their legs and head inside their shell.

A baby sea turtle would easily fit in the palm of your hand.

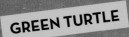

GREEN TURTLE

Trouble for Sea Turtles

Sea turtles are in danger!

Sometimes they mistake ocean
trash for food. Eating trash,
especially plastic, harms
sea turtles.

GREEN TURTLE

Others get caught in fishing nets by mistake and drown because they aren't able to come to the surface for air.

LOGGERHEAD

LEATHERBACKS

Another problem is light. Baby sea turtles emerge from their nests at night, then race toward the far-off, dim light where the sky meets the water. That's how they know where the ocean is! But if lights from homes and businesses are too close, the babies scurry toward them and away from the ocean.

We're Helping!

Many people are trying to help sea turtles. In some countries it is against the law to hurt a sea turtle or to bother eggs or nesting sites.

Many people with homes and businesses near nesting sites keep their lights off while babies are hatching.

A PROTECTED SEA TURTLE NEST IN FLORIDA, U.S.A.

DO NOT DISTURB
SEA TURTLE
NEST
VIOLATORS SUBJECT TO FINES
AND IMPRISONMENT

More and more fishers are using special nets that allow accidentally captured sea turtles to escape.

Special places called rehabilitation centers take in injured sea turtles. People care for them until they are well enough to return to the ocean.

How You Can Help

You don't have to be a scientist to help sea turtles. You don't even have to live near an ocean. All rivers flow to the sea, so cleaning up any river or stream helps keep plastic and other harmful trash out of the ocean.

Have a family cleanup party on a beach or waterfront near you!

YOU'LL NEED:

- a trash bag or bucket
- gloves
- at least one adult

Step 1: Put on your gloves.

Step 2: Walk along the water and pick up trash and place it in your trash bag or bucket.

Step 3: Put the trash into a marked garbage can or take it home with you for trash pickup.

Step 4: Have a picnic on your clean, beautiful beach or riverbank!

Feed the Sea Turtle

Some of these things are safe for turtles to eat. Some are not.

Use your finger to draw a line from safe foods to the turtle's mouth.

HAWKSBILL

Want to build your child's enthusiasm for sea turtles?

An aquarium is a great place to start. Most have at least one species of sea turtle. If you live near a coastal area or are considering a trip to one, you might also think about visiting a sea turtle rescue or rehabilitation center. Often, families can get a look at the important work going on behind the scenes and even participate in hand-feeding sea turtles. Here are some other activities for you and your child to do together.

Lots of Lunch! (Math)

Leatherbacks can eat their own weight in jellyfish each day. Help your child weigh themself. Then weigh one of their favorite foods. Divide your child's weight by the weight of the food to help them imagine how much of it they'd have to eat to equal their own weight. Talk about why it wouldn't be healthy for them to eat that much, even though a sea turtle can!

Turtle Bread
(Cooking and Measuring)

Go online and search for a turtle bread recipe. You'll find many options for a quick and simple turtle-shaped loaf of bread that you and your child can create—and enjoy!—together.

Tell Me a Story
(Storytelling)

Ask your child to imagine they're a brave-but-tiny baby sea turtle looking for ocean adventures. Build a story together, taking turns answering this question: "And what happens next?"

Track a Turtle
(Science)

Select a turtle from this Sea Turtle Conservancy website: conserveturtles.org/sea-turtle-tracking-active-sea-turtles. Find "your" turtle's current location, then check in from time to time, especially during the spring and summer nesting season. Notice how far females travel to lay eggs at the same beaches where they were hatched.

Make a Sea Turtle
(Craft)

Draw a simple turtle head and flippers on green construction paper. Have your child cut them out. Glue them under the edges of an upside-down paper bowl to create a turtle. Have your child paint the turtle's shell in colorful patterns to resemble scutes.

GLOSSARY

algae: simple plantlike organisms that use the sun to make food for themselves

clutch: a group of sea turtle eggs within a nest

currents: water streams moving through larger bodies of water

hatchling: a baby turtle just out of its eggshell

keratin: the material that makes up claws, feathers, fingernails, hair, hoofs, horns, scales, and scutes

mollusk: an animal with a soft body that usually lives inside a hard shell

predators: animals that hunt and eat other animals for food

rehabilitation: the process of bringing a sick or injured person or animal back to health

reptiles: animals with dry, scaly skin that lay eggs on land

scutes: protective platelike scales that cover a turtle's bony shell

sea sponge: an ocean animal that lives attached to something else, and has a body with many tiny holes that let food in and out

For Leo —J.E.

Cover, David Carbo/Shutterstock; back cover, Richard Carey/Adobe Stock; 1, Shane Myers Photography/Shutterstock; 5, Aquanaut4/Dreamstime; 6, M Swiet Productions/Getty Images; 7 (LE), Andrey Armyagov/Shutterstock; 7 (RT), Christine Wehrmeier/Getty Images; 10, Doug Perrine/Blue Planet Archive; 11, Ariadne Van Zandbergen/Getty Images; 12-13, Rich Carey/Shutterstock; 14, Jean-Paul Ferrero/AUSCAPE; 14-15, SeaTops/Blue Planet Archive; 16 (UP LE), Doug Perrine/Blue Planet Archive; 16 (UP RT), John Warburton-Lee Photography/Alamy Stock Photo; 16 (LO), Hector Chenge; 17 (UP LE), Hans Leijnse/Minden Pictures; 17 (UP RT), Burcet Sophie/Dreamstime; 17 (LO LE), Luiz Claudio Marigo/Minden Pictures; 17 (LO RT), Jim Abernethy/National Geographic Image Collection; 18-19, Brian J. Skerry/National Geographic Image Collection; 20, Doug Perrine/Minden Pictures; 21 (LE), Reinhard Dirscherl/Getty Images; 21 (RT), Ralph Pace/Minden Pictures; 22, J.W.Alker/Alamy Stock Photo; 23 (LE), Adam Butler/Blue Planet Archive; 23 (RT), Doug Perrine/Blue Planet Archive; 24-25, Jurgen Freund/Minden Pictures; 26, Jurgen Freund/Minden Pictures; 27, George H.H. Huey/Alamy Stock Photo; 28-29, Jurgen Freund/Minden Pictures; 31, Tony Bosse/Dreamstime.com; 32 (LE), Martin Demmel/Getty Images; 32 (RT), Rosemary Calvert/Getty Images; 33 (LE), Dai Mar Tamarack/Shutterstock; 33 (CTR), David Evison/Shutterstock; 33 (RT), Andrey Nekrasov/imagequestmarine.com; 34-35, M Swiet Productions/Getty Images; 36, Steve De Neef/National Geographic Image Collection; 37 (LE), J. Carlos Calvín/Alamy Stock Photo; 37 (RT), Jurgen Freund/Minden Pictures; 38, Ilka Cole/U.S. Air Force; 39, Joe Raedle/Getty Images; 41, David Pereiras/Shutterstock; 42, Rich Carey/Shutterstock; 43 (seaweed), Jiang Hongyan/Shutterstock; 43 (bag), Andrey/Adobe Stock; 43 (crab), Cheattha/Adobe Stock; 43 (straw), prapann/Adobe Stock; 43 (wrapper), springtime78/Shutterstock; 43 (jellyfish), MediaProduction/Getty Images

Designed by Kathryn Robbins

Hardcover ISBN: 978-1-4263-7158-5
Reinforced library binding ISBN: 978-1-4263-7159-2

The publisher would like to thank Dr. Karen A. Bjorndal for lending her expertise on this animal. The publisher would also like to thank Angela Modany, associate editor; Sarah J. Mock and Nicole DiMella, photo editors; Mike McNey, map production; Anne LeongSon and Gus Tello, design production assistants; and Joan Gossett, production editor.

Printed in Hong Kong
21/PPHK/1